G000150745

DID
YOUR
DAY
COUNT?

Learn to get more direction and
balance in your life!

SIOBHAN SIMS

SSC Publishing
Ireland
First published in Ireland by SSC Publishing 2010

1st Edition

Printed by Martins The Printers

Happy Reading!

CONTENTS

Dedication	1
My Appreciation	2
Why read this book?	3

LET'S START WITH DIRECTION!
- What is Your Plan?	7
- Have a Vision	9
- Chart Your Success	12
- Get a Diary	15
- Prioritise Your Life	17
- The Story of Your Life	19
- What Do You Love About Your Life Now?	21
- Why Are You Doing It?	23
- Plan Your Rewards	26
- Is Your Goal in Tune?	28
- Make Now the Right Time	29
- Believe in Yourself	31
- List Your Talents	33
- Everyone Has A Choice	35
- Let Go of Your Past	37
- Who Do You Want To Be?	39
- What Would You Do?	41

- What Are You Doing? 43
- Tools Are Good 45
- Have a Support Group 46
- Let Everyone Know 47
- A Bumpy Ride 49
- Know Who You Are 51
- Create Your Soundtrack 53

NOW FOR THE BALANCE
- Is Your Life Balanced? 56
- Make Every Day Special 59
- What Do You Do On Your Day Off? 61
- Sort Out Your Money 63
- You Will Need Energy 65
- Take Time To Think 67
- Feed Your Soul 69
- Squeeze The Fun Out Of Each Day! 70
- Clear The Clutter 72
- Create A Masterpiece 74
- Family Matters 75
- Will You Have Done Your Bit? 77
- Learn A New Skill 79
- Check Your Stress 81
- Sharing is Caring 83

- Don't Forget your Loved One 85
- What Are You Waiting For? 87
- Be Present In All You Do 89
- Learn to Relax 90
- Stop Thinking, Start Acting 92
- Have A Little Faith 94
- Are You All or Nothing? 96
- Surround Yourself With Positive People 98
- What Are You Collecting? 100
- Hold a "Friend Appreciation Night"! 102
- What have you learned today? 104
- Ask For Help! 106
- Go Easy On Yourself 107

FREE MINI-BOOK: Setting Goals That Work!

- Introduction 110
- Setting S.M.A.R.T. Goals 111
- Resources 119
- About the Susie Long Hospice Fund 122
- Notes Page 125

DEDICATION

I dedicate this book to the following people:

My friends, who have pushed me to get the book done and stop talking about it!

My family, who constantly tell me I can do it, and my parents who brought me up to believe in myself and nourished my ability to do anything I put my mind to.

Last, but not least, to my wonderful husband, Brian, who has supported me and supplied me with endless hugs through the journey of this book. I love you always xoxo

MY APPRECIATION

Thank you to all who have inspired me to write this book and given me the time to talk out my ideas and plans. Especially to Khan and Helena, who have given me the time to follow my dream.

I also want to thank Maeve Butler, not only for her inspiring work with the Susie Long Hospice Fund but also for her help with the finishing touches to the book.

This book is for anyone that has ever felt that a goal was too big, or has been told it was not worth it. I am proving to you now that it can be done. It may take longer than you wanted or even expected, but it will get done.

WHY READ THIS BOOK?

I am not famous. I have not climbed a mountain. I have jumped in a lake. I don't have a television show. I have gone through my share of problems just like everyone else. I have not always made the right choices. But, I am happy and healthy and have written this book for you. I have even included a FREE minibook in the back of this book called "Setting Goals That Work", to give you that extra support and help.

I have included 52 tips to getting balance and direction in your life and you may choose to take one a week and put it into practice.

Buying this book was, for some, a choice. A choice to stop complaining about the life you don't have and start doing something about it. I know, because I was one of those people and all I can say is "Congratulations!" and I hope you have as much fun as I did in executing that choice.

For others, you will be supporting the Susie Long Hospice Fund which receive €1.00 per book sold. My aim is to sell a million books so that they may have a €1,000,000 for their mission, their goal.

So on behalf of myself and the Susie Long Hospice Fund, we thank you for choosing to support both of us. For more on the Susie Long Hospice Fund and to make further donations, please check out their website:

www.susielonghospice.com

If you would like, you can contact me on the book website:

www.didyourdaycount.com

If you have any questions or inspiring stories, or just want to tell me how the book was for you, please feel free to drop me a line.

Stay positive and loving,

Siobhan Sims

Let's Start With The Direction!

WHAT IS YOUR PLAN?

Do you know where you are going in life?
You wouldn't hop in your car, pop on your
blindfold and head off to do the shopping,
would you?

No, of course not! You would get in the car
and head in the direction of the shops either
from memory of how to get there or look it up
on a map. As of today, I am asking you to take
off the blindfold to life and find your
direction. There is a minibook in the back of
this book that I have added for free in order to
help you draw your effective roadmap.

To some this sounds boring and I remember

thinking the same when I first thought of doing it. Then I realised, that I was so much happier, healthier and positive when I had direction in my life.

Giving your life direction does not mean you are going to be stuck to a routine everyday of your life with no spontaneity. In fact, it gives you the time to be spontaneous and have fun while still aiming for your dreams.

Now that doesn't sound too bad!

HAVE A VISION

Every morning, I take a few moments to imagine the life I want and to feel the way it would feel to have achieved it. I'm not talking about totally changing my life; I mean making a few improvements to the things I am not so happy about.

Visioning is one of the most effective ways to keep motivated when you are not feeling enthusiastic about your goal.

This is how it goes:

- Sit or stand comfortably and imagine yourself walking into a room.

- You will see yourself having achieved what

you are aiming for, whether it is losing 20Ibs or opening your own bookshop. This is the "Achieving You".

- People are around you and telling you how proud they are of you and telling you "Well done!"

- Notice how you are standing? I always see myself standing taller and shoulders back, but relaxed.

- What is the Achieving You wearing? How are you moving?

- Now, go forward and step into the Achieving You for a moment. FEEL the amazing feelings. HEAR what people are saying. Use all your senses to get yourself in there.

- Take some time and notice how amazing it feels and how motivated you feel.
- Make this the first thing you do every morning and feel yourself charge ahead towards your goal.

It feels brilliant, doesn't it?

CHART YOUR SUCCESS

How will you know that you have achieved your goal? Or how will you know that you have not left out a step along the way that may be vital to you completing your mission? This is your "YOU MUST DO" when it comes to goals. What you must do is:

- Find a large sheet of paper, the larger the better. You may need several sheets, depending on the duration of your goal.

- Draw up a chart, just like a calendar, with plenty of space for each date. A sheet per month works well for me.

- I normally draw up the next 2 months so as

to have a view ahead. This is also good for planning occasions. Remember, this will also be a chart for your life balance, which I will discuss later.

- After you have decided and planned out your goal, you will want to enter the steps on the dates you have charted.

- I always put in a space for rewards after having completed a step. This is so you celebrate and really take note of your achievements along your journey. It can be anything that you really want like a massage, a flying lesson or putting some money in the holiday fund. It doesn't matter as long as it is something you REALLY want and do not usually have. A real treat! Anything, as long as you celebrate your achievements on your journey.

What will your first step be?

How will you reward yourself?

GET A DIARY

It is not so easy to remember all our achievements when we are having a bad day and not feeling so good about ourselves. Get a diary and write these in it each night:

- 10 good deeds I did in my day
- 5 things I'm happy to have done today
- 3 things I learned in the day
- 5 things I wish I had got done in my day

Some days, I'm not able to answer all of the above, but at least it makes me look at my life a bit more closely and makes me more aware of what I want to do the next day. It also feels really good to read back on it a year later. It's amazing how easy it is to forget all the good things that happen in a day.

If you bring your attention to all the good in your life, it leaves little time to focus on the not so good.

PRIORITISE YOUR LIFE

It baffles me how, everyday, we give such importance to things that are not helping us achieve our dreams. Imagine what you could achieve if you transferred all that attention and time from e.g. watching one of the latest episodes of Coronation Street and instead aimed that time towards writing that first email to a publisher or taking one box of clutter from the study to sort through!

When I cut down my TV watching, I got my book finished, spent more time speaking to my friends and family, lost 20Ibs in weight and finally made a regular habit of meditation.

I want you to start thinking of areas where you could use your time more effectively. A one hour programme could be substituted for one hour of writing/knitting/an exercise DVD/doing a business plan/quality family time/learning a new recipe or simply some quiet time. One small change, one big reward. If you did that everyday, that would be around **365** hours a year that you were using to do something more fulfilling.

Makes you think, doesn't it?

THE STORY OF YOUR LIFE

This is an exercise that can allow the dreamer in you to emerge. I am asking you to write a magazine article about yourself with you having reached your intended goal. The article will tell of your life up to now and continue right up to when you reached your goal. Include the names of those who helped you along the way and those who inspired you. Imagine your picture alongside it. Make it as big as you wish. Think Bill Cullen or Oprah! It should be the best article ever written about you as you are the interviewer. Even if you feel you have not done much, write the future for yourself. Write about all the things you are going to do and how you will do them. This is your life!

The only person holding you back is you.

Remember, there is no-one who will have the same experiences as you in your life.

You are truly unique.

WHAT DO YOU LOVE
ABOUT YOUR LIFE NOW?

I have always observed that there are people who never seem to be happy with what they have and have no appreciation for how far they have come. They finally get the car they want and they want a bigger one. They buy a house and then spend days worrying about making it better. They win the lottery and end up bankrupt within a year. From now on, you are going to start and end each day being grateful and thankful for all you have. Thankful for the freedom to live by your own rules. Grateful for family, friends and loved ones. Thankful for the food you have and the possessions such as your phone, TV, books, computers and all the other gadgets which we take as the norm.

Gratitude makes life look better.

WHY ARE YOU DOING IT?

It is very easy to push and push towards a goal that you think you want, only to realise it is not what you really want at all. Whether it is a parent or a friend or someone you admired having wanted or achieved this same goal, it can become very hazy and before you know it, you are living someone else's dream. If this happens, it is not the end of the world. Trust me. This has happened to me and it is all a matter of looking at what you have learnt from the experience, dusting yourself off and then having a rethink on what it really is that you want from life. It is also important to look at what achieving this task would bring you, as that will help you decide what you really want.

- Do you want to be famous? If so, why?
- What will fame bring for you?
- Will it be acceptance?
- Will it be a feeling of importance?

Perhaps you just want people to know you have something to say which you may not have had a chance to express in your life so far.

Constantly questioning your reasons and breaking down the layers will not only give you insight to yourself, but will also help you to understand the feelings you have beneath the choices you are making.

Your choices and your knowledge are your power and responsibility.

PLAN YOUR REWARDS

If you keep on slogging ahead and never taking time to reward yourself or realise how great you are to have come this far, you may start to wonder what you are doing it all for. So, time to plan your reward or even **rewards**. I have already spoken about having your chart and having it split into steps. I also said you should have a reward section. Here are some examples:

- Spending a relaxing evening with your loved one!
- A new bottle of luxurious bubble bath

- A hot stone massage
- A week in a rental cottage by the sea

Now, it's time for you to plan your rewards!

1. _____

2. _____

3. _____

4. _____

5. _____

IS YOUR GOAL IN TUNE?

If your goal is not in tune with your life, beliefs and ethics, it is not going to make you happy. That is why you need to believe that your goal is not only helping you, but the world, too.

If your goal is to make a line of ethical clothes at affordable prices, yet you are using sweat shops to make them, that is just not going to fit with your life and will leave you feeling guilty and not right in yourself.

MAKE NOW THE RIGHT TIME

As a life coach, I have heard my fair share of excuses as to why goals are not working. None of them matter. What matters is making the choice to do it NOW.

Procrastination will have you putting all your tinned food in alphabetical order before doing the things that really matter. I know, as it used to be my very favourite thing to do around exam time instead of studying. My parents had a very clean house around exam time!

Go and look at your chart and take the next step of your goal. If you can't do that, find another step you could be doing.

When you make excuses, you are only fooling yourself. So as of today, you are a No Excuse person and are going to be true to yourself. Feel the power of making that promise to yourself and see the results of your progress.

Your new mantra:

I am a No Excuse person!

BELIEVE IN YOURSELF

This is one thing that most people don't like to think or talk about as they feel embarrassed. They are afraid they may be seen as being cocky or proud, which is completely different to having self-belief. People who are cocky or proud are often those who have no self-belief and put on a veneer.

If one of your goals is to start a new business or choose a new career, you need to believe in yourself before you can make others believe in you.

I would like you to make a list of at least 50 things you have achieved in your life. I know it sounds like a lot, but you don't have to do it all in one go.

I also want you to think of times when you did something that scared you. You would not believe the self-belief and confidence that emerges from tackling a fear. Now there is a thin line between courageous and stupid!

Grabbing a poisonous snake in a non-controlled condition = stupid.

Boarding a plane while afraid of flying = courageous.

Just so you know the difference!

LIST YOUR TALENTS

You are the most valuable possession needed to achieve your goal. Your talents may be what has led you to what you want to achieve, or maybe you have always known where you want to go but are not sure how you are going to get there. This is where your list of talents will help you.

I am looking for you to make a list of at least 20 of your talents and I want it on a piece of paper that is going to be with you at all times. You are going to read through this every morning while having your breakfast. Anytime you have a problem, you are going to read it again and you can even add to it as you get more direction in your life.

Remember, "Being a good friend" and "fun to be with", are classified talents!

Now, start thinking and start writing: you may be surprised with some of the things you come up with.

List five of your talents:

1. _____

2. _____

3. _____

4. _____

5. _____

EVERYONE HAS A CHOICE

I know at times you feel you do not have a choice. You'll tell yourself:

- I can't leave my job.
- I can't leave an abusive relationship.
- I can't take that risk.
- I could never be a good parent.
- I'm not in control of the situation.
- I have to smoke/drink/take drugs. I'm addicted.

You ALWAYS have a choice. You have a choice to ask for help.

You may not like the options 100%, but you still have a choice. You may be afraid of the other option but, guess what, you still have a choice. This is your life and your life is your responsibility. Make that choice right now.

What you do in your life is your choice.

LET GO OF YOUR PAST

Is your past following you around like a black cloud? Is there someone that is constantly with you in your mind and affecting the way you live in the moment? These may be people that made you feel less than great about yourself, or an occasion that has haunted you and your self-belief.

It is time to let them go

Write them a letter or scribble down the bad experience that is haunting you and burn it. If you need help, seek a professional counsellor or psychiatrist to help with the burden.

By living in your past, you are missing all the great things happening to you in the present.

If you are constantly looking in the rear view mirror, there is a chance you are going to crash!

WHO DO YOU WANT TO BE?

Do you portray the image of the person you want to be? You wouldn't walk around your office in your pyjamas if you wanted to be seen as an important and successful business person! So take some time and picture yourself as the person you want to be, and what you would look like from your head to your toes. Then start to integrate that into your life. You may need help from a stylish friend or even an image consultant. You may pull out pictures of people you aspire to be (make sure they are modern magazines and not ones from the '70s!) and go to a personal shopper. Most department stores have personal shoppers and, best of all, they are FREE.

Remember, you are not aiming to be a clone of your role model. You are simply aiming to improve your already wonderful self!

WHAT WOULD YOU DO?

What would you do if you knew you could not fail? Imagine, without a doubt, you were going to succeed and nothing could stop you. You may imagine exactly the life you have and would not change a thing. However, you may imagine a very different route and want to change your entire existence. We hear it everyday, people giving up the rat race and buying a small vineyard in the South of France or giving up the high flying job in London to teach yoga in Donegal. They may be living more frugally, but I bet they are happier than they have ever been because they are following the path they have yearned for. So ask yourself, what would you REALLY be doing if you followed your heart?

List five things you would do if you knew you could not fail:

1. _____

2. _____

3. _____

4. _____

5. _____

WHAT ARE YOU DOING?

Sometimes, we feel we are doing loads but getting nowhere near our goal and this can be very disheartening. In fact, it can often make people stop working towards their goal and leave them feeling that they have failed.

If you even start to feel that this is happening, I want you to STOP! Stop and ask yourself, "What am I doing?"

Are you still working to your priorities? Are you putting more energy into things that are not part of the big picture? More than likely, you will find that you went off track along the way. However, the good news is that you can go back to your chart and pick up from where you veered off, knowing that you didn't stray far and now know what you are doing!

Always keep an eye on your goal.

TOOLS ARE GOOD

Tools could be computers, scanners, printers, gym gear, anything that helps you with your goal. There are no rules when it comes to this. You can borrow, rent or even get a donation of something. On www.gumtree.ie, people give things away everyday which others want. Put up a listing for what you want and start thinking outside the box.

Could your friends or family help you?

HAVE A SUPPORT GROUP

I don't mean "My name is Siobhan Sims and I'm a chocoholic". When heading on the journey of a big goal, it is really important to have someone you can talk things out with or someone to tell you "You can do it!" when you are feeling less than confident about your direction.

However, this does not always fall to your friends, family or significant other; It may mean getting professional help from a life coach, even a counsellor if it is a more deeply-rooted issue.

LET EVERYONE KNOW

Too many people keep problems that need solving to themselves. I find this complete madness; as by sharing a problem, you may find a better solution or even better, have many solutions to choose from. For example, I was looking for premises for my life coaching practice when I first started out, and when I mentioned it to someone I happened to be speaking to at the bank, they knew someone who had just had an office become available. Problem solved.

Also, family and friends are great for helping with problems, especially younger members as they think more courageously and innovatively.

If there is no-one around and you need to sort a problem out, I always get a large piece of paper, write the problem at the top of the sheet and then let my brain go mad. Write down everything, no matter how crazy it is and you would be amazed what you come up with. This exercise has not failed me yet!

A problem shared, is a problem solved!

A BUMPY RIDE

Things do not always go to plan, even when we have our charts drawn and our goal within reaching distance. Life happens. This book has been in the making for the past six years and has hit road bumps along the way that were unavoidable. However, if this happens, remember to breathe and know that all is not lost. Two years ago, my grandmother died and, being the first person to die who was close to me, I was overtaken by grief. Her loss filled me and all else was blinkered from my vision. Then one day, life just fell back into place and I continued with my goal. Here in your hands is the proof that you can still go on, even if you left the path for a short part of the journey.

Never lose hope in your goal and yourself.

KNOW WHO YOU ARE

Think of this as a first date with someone you cannot lie to!

I want you to sit down and answer some of these questions:

- What song would describe your life?
- What is your idea of a perfect day out?
- What is your favourite film and why?
- What would you choose as your last 3-course meal?
- If you were to win an award, what would it be for?
- What would be a dream come true for you?
- What would you do if you did not have to

worry about money?

- What inspirational figure would you like to have dinner with and what life lesson would they tell you?

My friends and I play this the whole time and it's great to not only learn about each other, but you really think about yourself. Fun for all the family!

Next question please!

CREATE YOUR SOUNDTRACK

Music is not everyone's cup of tea, but you have to admit that emotions and feelings can be raised with the first few notes of a recognised song. The song you danced your heart out to on the night of your debs. The first song at your wedding. The song that you and all your friends sang at the top of your lungs on a road trip to Kerry! So when you are feeling less than inspired and need some energy or simply to remember a good time, put together a few songs that make you feel like flinging up your arms and dancing your socks off. This will be your soundtrack to a

happier and more fun life and will keep you
dancing along the path you are taking.

List ten songs for your soundtrack:

1. _____

2. _____

3. _____

4. _____

5. _____

6. _____

7. _____

8. _____

9. _____

10. _____

NOW

FOR

THE

BALANCE!

IS YOUR LIFE BALANCED?

Generally, when people think their life is unbalanced, they tend to blame one thing as opposed to looking at the whole picture. This is a rough dividing up of your life:

1. Family   _____

2. Work   _____

3. Money   _____

4. Spirituality   _____

5. Romance/Partner   _____

6. Friends   _____

7. Belongings   _____

8. Health   _____

9. Personal Development   _____

10. Personal Care/YOU time   _____

Why not grade your life at this moment, giving each area a score between 1 and 10, 1 being bad and 10 being amazing.

Do not be alarmed if there are a few low scores. This is natural and means at least now you know where to start making changes in order to return your life to balance heaven.

If you have a score between 8 and 10, find out where those 2 points went to and keep a gentle eye on that area. Anything less than 8 and you need to look at what has caused the drop. Once you figure this out, write down what you need to do and write these new steps into your diary at specific dates and times. Example: You have let your friends slip away. Ring them and organise a set date and time to catch up. It can be simply calling over for tea or calling and chatting on the phone but make it an official and lasting change.

Before you know it, balance will be restored!

MAKE EVERY DAY SPECIAL

Do you wait until the weekend to call a friend or a relation? Do you wait until holidays to spend quality time with your kids? Do you think one day out of the whole 365 days of the year is enough to give flowers and chocolate? Your mission, should you choose to accept it, is to make every day special and show appreciation to those who support you and love you.

You might do some of the following:

- Buy a bunch of flowers when doing your weekly shop

- Have a dinner party just for your family - All three courses!
- Buy a box of chocolates for someone who helps you, such as your dry cleaner or your child minder

List five things that could make your day a special day:

1. _____
2. _____
3. _____
4. _____
5. _____

WHAT DO YOU DO ON YOUR DAY OFF?

Most people spend their day off running from one thing to the next and spending no time on themselves. I dare you to have a day of doing things you love to do. Rent a movie you've been dying to see. Start working through that pile of books. Treat yourself to lunch. Do something just for you.

You deserve it. It's your life!

You may also take this time to take one of those baby steps towards reaching your goal. It may be making a phone call, talking to a specialist or sending off a letter. Every bit helps and will make you feel confident that you are heading in the right direction.

Write down what your dream day off would be like:

_____

_____

_____

_____

_____

_____

SORT OUT YOUR MONEY

It is very easy to think if you ignore your money problems, they will go away. In fact, they will only get worse. So, if money is a problem, you need to get someone who can help you. You really have no excuse as there are some great FREE organisations out there that can help you towards budgeting and overcoming debt. I have listed some contact details in the back of the book to help you. When I was looking at my goal, I knew I was going to need money. So I made a saving plan and focused my attention on what I could do while saving. That way, I was not stuck waiting for something or someone and feeling like I was not getting anywhere. So just move on to the next step towards your goal while keeping an eye on your money.

List five ways you could cut back on your spending:

1. _____
2. _____
3. _____
4. _____
5. _____

YOU WILL NEED ENERGY

I know, it's been a long day at the office and the thought of getting into a pair of tracksuit bottoms for anything other than lying on the sofa, like hitting the treadmill or going for a walk, is the last thing on your mind.

Remember how good you feel after getting out and exercising? Feel all the energy it gives you and how much more relaxed it makes you, and just do it.

It doesn't have to be conventional exercise like the gym or running. For example:

- You could turn on your favourite tunes and dance freely around the sitting room.

- Jump around on the trampoline.
- Use hand weights while watching your favourite programme.

How are you going to add more exercise into your life? List five ways:

1. _____
2. _____
3. _____
4. _____
5. _____

TAKE TIME TO THINK

It is so important to take just 10 minutes a day in peace and silence with yourself to hear yourself think and feel. Between work, family and friend commitments, it is often quite hard to find time for yourself, but before you can help anyone else, you need to look after YOU!

- I use the bathroom as it is the one place you have an excuse to lock the door and take as long as you want.
- Maybe go out to your car on your morning break and just close your eyes and focus on your breathing.

- Be first up in the morning and take a few minutes to relax and focus on your breathing
- Take 10 minutes in the car before stepping through your front door after work.

When is your quiet time?

FEED YOUR SOUL

Are you eating the right foods? Are you constantly forcing your body through detoxes and diets or binges and boredom eating? Only you can answer this honestly. Stop and listen to your body. Consult a professional if you need help with your diet. Imagine all you will save on doctor, dental and food bills.

A healthy body means a healthy mind and that will mean:

- Thinking more quickly on your feet
- Finding solutions more easily
- Having more energy and less stress

What's not to love!

SQUEEZE THE FUN
OUT OF EACH DAY!

It seems that some people have forgotten to laugh or even smile. I know for some it seems beyond belief, whether they are suffering from chronic pain or even bereavement, but a smile is proven to make you feel better. It has been scientifically proven, but I won't bore you with that!

You don't even have to be smiling at anything in particular; just putting a smile on your face can make you feel uplifted, happier and even optimistic.

Your task:

Remember something you used to love to do as a child, whether it is building something with Lego (my favourite) or colouring in. Do it now. No-one's watching!

CLEAR THE CLUTTER

Clutter does not mean that your house is dirty. Clutter is stuff filling space that could be used for you to live. If you feel a panic attack coming on as soon as you step into your study, you need to clear the clutter. You may have to hire someone to help you forge your way through it, or ask a friend who has been begging you to let them at it. Either way, the clutter needs to go and that means for all your areas: Your kitchen, your bedroom and your work area. If your area is cluttered, your mind will be cluttered and that is not going to help you. It surely cannot be helping you at work. So start a box at a time and be a bit ruthless. If you have not missed something for six months, let it go.

Where are you going to start?

CREATE A MASTERPIECE

Most of us don't have the luxury of exploring and using our creative side in our everyday life. That is why it is all the more important to allocate some time each day to creating something, whether it is trying out a new recipe, painting a picture or making a rocking chair, despite never having done woodwork. Whatever you choose, it is essential that you have fun doing it! You may have a genuine gift for whichever craft you choose. I know plenty of people who have taken their hobby and turned it into a business. I sell the earrings I make on EBay! What will you do?

FAMILY MATTERS

It is easy to think that your family will always be there, but we can never have that guarantee. So don't forget to phone home if you can't visit once in a while. Even sending an email or messaging a family member on Facebook is better than no contact at all. You'll miss them when they are gone and wish you had spent more time with them.

Since my family live in Co. Clare and I in Kilkenny, we don't see each other as often as we would like. Sundays are our catch-up days without fail, so we make time to keep up to date with each other. Since we are a busy family, a phone call works well for us and at least we are letting each other know that we are thinking of each other, even if we can't be in the same place at the same time.

Who have you been neglecting lately? Go give them a call!

WILL YOU HAVE DONE YOUR BIT?

It doesn't have to be much. Switch off the lights when you leave a room, don't leave your appliances on stand-by. Don't leave the tap running while brushing your teeth. All these things are small but can make a big difference if everyone does their bit. A lot of people think, "What difference can I make as I am only one person?" I say if everyone does their little bit, it could make a huge difference to the overall picture. Think of it as payback to the planet for giving us amazing sunrises and sunsets, beautiful green trees, adorable creatures that roam our gardens and amazing clear skies so we can gaze at the stars on warm nights. I think being a little bit greener is a small price to pay for such beauty.

What one thing could you do to

make a difference?

LEARN A NEW SKILL

This does not mean you have to go back to college and get your Masters or collect certificates and diplomas. I want you to consider all the things you would love to learn to do, whether it's cooking Chinese or learning how to take the perfect photograph. There are some great evening courses available these days, from looking up your family history to car mechanics. You can even buy a book about a topic that has always interested you and learn something new. There is also a fountain of knowledge on the internet about everything from how to apply the perfect makeup to building your own chest of drawers. Be adventurous and you'd be amazed where it will take you. After all, when you stop learning, you stop living.

What skill could you learn to make life that bit more interesting?

CHECK YOUR STRESS

Setting a goal and deciding to be responsible for your future can be a big undertaking. It may lead to much change and, for some, a completely new life. A real adventure! However, do make sure to keep the balance in your life and make sure you do not give yourself too short a timeline to achieve your goal or set yourself too much to do at one time. Remember, this is meant to be fun and a joy to do. You don't want to end up resenting having to give up time with friends and family to achieve your goal; that would not be balanced and would go against the whole purpose of your striving to achieve direction and balance in your life. So make sure to put time aside so you can have some "**you**" time to relax and enjoy the fruits of your labour.

Don't forget to breathe…………..

SHARING IS CARING

It is all too easy to get caught up in our days and not think of those who need help around us. Whether it is helping out at a homeless shelter or calling in on a mature neighbour who may need groceries or some turf carried in, there are plenty of ways to reach out a hand. Identifying your talents and using them in your community can often be the best of both worlds. Not only are you keeping a talent from gathering dust within you, you are also helping others and everyone knows how great it feels to give to others without expecting anything in return. I also feel it is important, as it helps you to be more connected with your community and allows you to contribute to the greater good.

Open your eyes and see how you can make a difference!

DON'T FORGET YOUR LOVED ONE

It is very easy to get caught up in work, children, hobbies and family. That's why it is all the more important to spend quality time with your loved one away from everyday responsibilities.

This allows you to:

- Show your appreciation of each other.
- Get back in touch with each other.
- Fall in love all over again!

Set a day aside each week where you spend an evening together. It doesn't have to cost you a penny. It could be a walk in the park or cooking a nice meal together. The important part is that you put in the effort, have fun and relax with each other.

When did you last tell your loved one you were so thankful for all they do for you?

WHAT ARE YOU WAITING FOR?

Are you always telling yourself you'll be happy when:

- You lose weight?
- You get the perfect car?
- You own the big house?
- You are dating the perfect man/woman?
- You get the right job?
- You get that big promotion?

Why are you not allowing yourself to be happy right now? Why are you punishing yourself? Do you not feel you deserve to be happy? I am telling you now, you deserve to be happy.

Say it to yourself "I deserve to be happy" and keep saying it till you believe it!

What would help you to believe that you are deserving of happiness in your life?

BE PRESENT IN ALL YOU DO

I find this the most important. Have you ever been talking to someone and then realised that they were miles away and didn't hear a word you were saying? I know, I hate it too. So let's not do the same. If you are with family, be with family. If you are at work, be at work. You'll be more productive and, in turn, happier during your downtime. If I feel I am starting to lose my focus, I notice my hands. I slowly rub the back of one hand with the fingers of the other and focus on the feeling. Very soon, you will find yourself present in all you do without even having to try.

LEARN TO RELAX

Some people like to meditate as a way of chilling out, others like a bit of escapism at the cinema. I now want you to make a list of at least seven different ways that you yourself could relax. Choose ways to relax that take less time to do during the busy working week, and a few different ways that take longer for over the weekend.

Here are a few ideas which I personally use:

1. A hot bath with aromatherapy oils
2. Sitting on my beanbag listening to a meditation CD

3. Using a steam room or sauna at the local fitness centre

4. Losing myself in a good book!

5. 10 minutes of gentle stretching with relaxing music

What 3 ways could help you to relax?

1. _____

2. _____

3. _____

STOP THINKING, START ACTING

No point sitting there thinking about going to the gym and mentally talking yourself out of it. Just pack your gear and walk out the door, get in the car and drive to the gym. Before you know it, you'll actually look forward to going and feeling great.

The same goes with a big task. When you break it down into small pieces and allocate a time to do it, you are more likely to complete your task. You will feel proud of yourself for taking another chunk off your goal, as opposed to looking at this huge mountain you have to climb and feeling the weakness in your legs before you have even taken the first step.

Preparation is essential in making <u>confident</u> steps towards your goal!

HAVE A LITTLE FAITH

When I say the word faith, some people's first image is religion. This is an area I tend to steer clear of as religion means so many things to so many people and there are so many different beliefs.

In this instance, I'm not referring to religion. I am talking about faith in yourself and your ability. Faith in people around you and faith that people want the best for you. Faith that no matter what happens in life, it will all work out for the best.

Faith for me is what keeps me going when I am on the edge of giving up and have lost a bit of my direction. Faith is what keeps me believing in myself and my abilities.

What does faith mean to you?

ARE YOU ALL OR NOTHING?

I have to admit, I used to be this type of person at one time, until I realised I was getting nowhere and was becoming very inflexible. I wouldn't go to the gym unless I had at least two hours. This often meant that I never made it to the gym as I was so rigid with my time. I now do small 15 minute intervals of exercise that fit into my day and I plan them out on my chart. That is why the chart is so important: it helps you to still reach your result, but you are doing it in smaller steps that you can fit into your life. By doing this, you don't pressurise yourself with unrealistic expectations leaving you stressed and unbalanced trying to get things done.

Are you an all-or-nothing person?

SURROUND YOURSELF
WITH POSITIVE PEOPLE

I know this has been said a thousand times but it really is the most important thing you can do for yourself. Putting yourself in negative situations, such as visiting a relative that is always putting you down or putting up with a friend who is trying to sabotage your plans, is madness. There are more and more positive groups of people than ever meeting to discuss life goals and life changes, and there are also several online support forums that are great, too! I also got my friends involved in finding a goal which means that we can support each other and keep upbeat and positive. For some inspiration, visit **www.43things.com,** a website where people list their goals, offer suggestions and support each other.

How many positive people do you have in your life?

WHAT ARE YOU COLLECTING?

Are you collecting material goods? Now, more than ever, with the recession, it is ludicrous to spend money on the latest car, style accessory or material item that depreciates in value and is the equivalent of throwing money away!

I have always been keen on the idea of collecting memories instead of material goods. Travel is one of the best ways of doing this. Not just abroad, but around Ireland, too. I always write a journal at the end of each day, so that in years to come I can relive the journey over again. For others it may be family times spent together. Whatever your experience of choice, make it a truly valuable one and one that will appreciate with time.

What would you like to collect

more of in your life?

HOLD A "FRIEND APPRECIATION" NIGHT!

I consider myself extremely lucky to have such good friends who I have known all my life and can call on, no matter what. We always make sure to appreciate our significant other at least once a year on Valentine's Day. We have Mother's Day and Father's Day and now it is time for Friend's Day.

Have a party with your closest friends and, at some stage of the night, ask each person to write their name on the top of a piece of paper. The sheets of paper are passed around the group and each has to write what they love about the person whose name is at the top. I remember doing this in school when I was 13 years old and I still have my sheet of paper to this day.

Start planning your night right now!

WHAT HAVE YOU LEARNED TODAY?

I am all about learning and expanding the mind with knowledge. Whether it's picking up a book and reading a bit on photography in the wild, or throwing on a CD to learn French while driving to work. It doesn't have to be a massive achievement or even be something essential, it may simply be something you have always wondered about and never gotten a chance to look into more deeply.

It could also be learning about how to do your job more efficiently. Whatever you choose, make sure it is enjoyable and that you come away feeling better about yourself and more confident having expanded your mind.

Think about your day and ask yourself, what have I learnt today?

ASK FOR HELP!

I have to admit, I have never been good at accepting that I cannot do something myself, but since I realised I can achieve my goal more efficiently and do a better job by asking for help, I have become a new found believer. Why flounder trying to do something that, frankly, you are not enjoying, when you can ask someone who is an expert? You may not even have to pay cash: you can exchange talents or professions. One hour of life coaching for one hour of web design.

Hey presto!

GO EASY ON YOURSELF

I want you think about what a truly best friend would be like? My list goes as follows:

- They would point out all the great things you are capable of doing and understand when you get it wrong
- They would be your friend no matter what
- They would never let someone treat you badly
- They would look after you when you needed to be taken care of.

Now, I want you to make YOU your new best friend. If, like me, you really have friends like the above, you are blessed. However, you still need to show yourself the same love and attention that you would a best friend.

You are only human.....

FREE MINIBOOK

SETTING

GOALS

THAT WORK!

INTRODUCTION

By now, you have read *Did Your Day Count?* and are ready to start making some choices. There are 5 stages to creating the perfect goal or what is commonly known as a S.M.A.R.T. goal.

S.M.A.R.T. stands for:
1. Specific
2. Measurable
3. Attainable
4. Relevant
5. Time-Sensitive

Stage 1

Specific

Whether your goal is to lose weight or start a business, you cannot just leave it vague.

If you are to lose weight, you need to specify how much you are looking to lose. So your new goal would sound like "My goal is to lose 20Ibs". If it's starting a business, you need to be more like "I want to start a small café selling yummy cakes and tea" or "I want to form a theatre company that performs amazing plays by up and coming writers".

Specific!

Stage 2

Measurable

You must have a way of seeing that your goal is making progress. So if your goal is to save money, you need to have a target amount to save and the time you will save it in, as well as an account or budget that can track how you're doing, otherwise you might find yourself going off-track in the sales!

So your goal could sound as follows: I will save €10,000 in three years in my credit union account.

Stage 3

Attainable

Your goal must be attainable from where you are now. Do you have what you need to achieve your goal? Is your goal realistic? Now I'm not being a pessimist, but an unrealistic goal such as "I am going to lose 30lbs in a healthy manner in 2 days", as I'm sure you would be told by a doctor, is impossible. A more attainable goal would sound like "I am going to lose 30lbs in a healthy manner over four months". So be realistic and, while it may take a bit longer, you'll have a greater chance of achieving your goal.

Stage 4

Relevant

Your goals have to be relevant to your life. If you have a goal like, "I am going to make a load of money robbing banks" but you believe that stealing is wrong, then you can see how it would not be relevant to your life. A more relevant goal for you might sound like, "I am going to make a load of money by getting a well-paid job". So make sure to check your goal against your ethics and beliefs, so that you can enjoy your success when it comes (and not get arrested)!

Stage 5

Time-sensitive

We all know that if we don't have to have something done by a particular deadline, we might be tempted to put it off, or procrastinate. A vague goal would be "I will write a book". A time-sensitive goal would be "I will write a book by the 1st January 2011". That way you have something definite to aim for, instead of a vague idea that has no direction.

At the end of the 5 stages:

A goal such as "I want to lose weight" would sound like "I want to lose 20lbs using a healthy diet and regular exercise by the 1st April 2011 and will lose 2lbs per week". Now that is a goal not to be messed with!

Write your goal now:

_____

_____

_____

_____

_____

Here are a few extra tips to help you on your way:

- Complete at least one action a day. One small step taken regularly can keep you chipping off chunks of your big goal. You'll be done before you know it!

- Plan rewards at every step of the progress and not just at the end of your achievement. If your goal is over five years, that is one hell of a wait and you may lose your motivation.

- Write each of your steps and tasks into your diary and give yourself a bit of flexibility, one or two hours, in getting them done in case of any unexpected delays.

- Keep an eye on your progress. One task not done here and a delay with one there can make a big difference in the long run, so it is best to keep an eye and be aware that you may have to change some things around in order to make up the progress.

- Do your research. You wouldn't start a course in primary school teaching before doing some work experience, would you? What if it turned out to not be what you wanted to do after all?

RESOURCES

Websites

There are several websites that can help you with tracking your goal, as well as getting help and advice from others.

These are some of my favourites:

- **www.43things.com**

A social networking site where users share lists of goals and hopes as well as giving advice on achieving goals.

- **www.joesgoals.com**

Joe's Goals is a simple yet powerful tool to make tracking your goals the easiest part of accomplishing them and it's free!

- **www.wesabe.com**

A money management tool which also provides the added bonus of community sharing and support.

- ## www.fitday.com

Free online diet and fitness journal.

- ## www.marblecityhealth.com

A network of complimentary therapists, health practitioners, fitness instructors and food producers based in and around Kilkenny.

- ## www.mabs.ie

MABS is an Irish, free, confidential and independent service for people in debt or in danger of getting into debt.

- ## www.nationaldebtline.co.uk

Free debt advice and support for people with money worries and debt problems in England, Wales & Scotland

- ## www.pueblo.gsa.gov

USA Federal Citizen Information Center - answers to your questions about the Federal government and common consumer issues as well as money issues.

Publications

Here are some publications I find useful and encouraging:

- **"Change Your Life in 7 Days" by Paul McKenna**
- **"Screw It, Just Do It" by Richard Branson**
- **"It's Not How Good You Are, It's How Good You Want To Be" by Paul Arden**
- **The Four Agreements by Don Miguel Ruiz**
- **Psychologies Magazine**

The Susie Long Hospice Fund was set up in October 2007 to provide the highest possible quality of end-of-life care for patients and their families through the establishment of a 10-bed hospice in Kilkenny, for the people of Kilkenny and Carlow.

The Fund is meeting this challenge through fundraising, increasing awareness of the need and benefits of local hospice care and by lobbying Government for support.

Donations can be made directly to the fund at:

AIB, High St, Kilkenny

Account No: 34627051

Sort code: 93-31-98

IBAN: IE70AIBK

SWIFT: AIBKIE2D

The Susie Long Hospice Fund is a registered charity, number CHY17950.

For more, check out their website:

www.susielonghospice.com

Siobhan Sims has the following CDs and books coming soon!

~ ~ ~ ~

Learning to Love Yourself:

A book on finding self-appreciation

~ ~ ~ ~

Journeys to Yourself:

A CD of meditations for self-discovery

~ ~ ~ ~

Stop the Stress & Start Living

A book to help you control stress in your life

~ ~ ~ ~

NOTES:

NOTES:

NOTES:

_____

_____

_____

_____

_____

_____

_____

_____

_____

_____

_____

_____

_____

_____

_____

NOTES:

NOTES:

NOTES: